CATS

by Michèle Dufresne

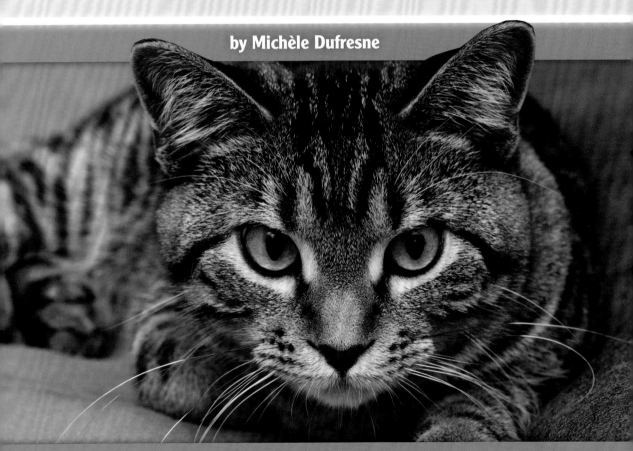

Pioneer Valley Educational Press, Inc.

TABLE OF CONTENTS

KINDS OF CATS

There are many kinds of cats.

Some cats are large.
Some cats are small.
Some cats are pets.
Some cats are wild animals.

We call the cats we keep as pets **domestic** cats. They come in many colors.

Some domestic cats have long fur, and some have short fur.

All cats have soft fur that keeps them warm.

WILD CATS

All cats, big and small, are called **felines**.

Here is a tiger. Tigers are the largest cats. Most tigers live in forests or grasslands.

A tiger's stripes help **camouflage** it in the wild so it can sneak up on its **prey**.

Lions are also very large cats.
This is a male lion.
He has a shaggy mane.
Female lions do not have manes.

The cheetah is another kind of cat.
The cheetah is the fastest animal on land.
It can run as fast as 70 miles per hour.
The cheetah uses its speed to catch its prey.

A bobcat is bigger than a house cat, but is smaller than most wild cats.

The bobcat hunts small prey and large prey.

This bobcat is watching its prey. ▶

DOMESTIC CATS

Many people keep cats as pets.

There are many different kinds
of domestic cats.

Here is a Siamese cat.
Siamese cats have blue eyes. ▶

Here is a Persian cat.
Persian cats have long fur.

Here is a tabby cat.
Tabby cats have
stripes or spots.

15

Cats like to sleep many hours each day. Most cats sleep lightly much of the time they are asleep. When cats are sleeping lightly, they can wake up very quickly.

We call this light sleeping a "catnap."

Cats love to climb.
Sometimes they climb up trees.

Sometimes a cat climbs too far
to jump down. Then the cat is stuck!
Someone with a big ladder has to help
the cat get down from the tree.

GROOMING

Most cats do not like baths.

Cats groom themselves.
They lick themselves clean with their tongues.
Their tongues are rough, like sandpaper.

KITTENS

Baby cats are called kittens. After they are born, their eyes are closed for about seven days. Newborn kittens stay close to their mother to stay warm. They drink their mother's milk for food.

Kittens grow fast.
They begin to eat by themselves.
They love to play and explore.

GLOSSARY

camouflage: to hide by looking like the background

domestic: tame, used to humans

feline: belonging to the cat family

prey: an animal hunted and killed by another animal for food

INDEX